612
War
c.1   Ward, Brian R.

The Brain and Nervous System

U.S.A

GRENADA   SPECIAL

21940

612
War
c.1   Ward, Brian R.

The Brain and Nervous System

Siskiyou County Schools Library
Yreka, California

THE BRAIN AND NERVOUS SYSTEM

Brian R. Ward

Series consultant:
Dr A. R. Maryon-Davis
MB, BChir, MSc, MRCS, MRCP

The Human Body

Franklin Watts
London New York Sydney Toronto

First published in Great Britain 1981 by
Franklin Watts Ltd
8 Cork Street
London W1

First published in the United States of America 1981
Franklin Watts Inc.
730 Fifth Avenue
New York
N.Y. 10019

UK ISBN: 0 85166 907 7
US ISBN: 0-531-04288-X
Library of Congress Catalog Card No: 80-54825

Designed by Howard Dyke

Acknowledgments

The illustrations were prepared by: Andrew Aloof, Marion
Appleton, Nick Cudworth, The Diagram Group, Howard
Dyke, David Holmes, David Mallott, Roy Wiltshire.

Contents

Introduction

What *is* the brain? And why do we need a nervous system?

Your brain is the most important single organ in your body. It controls everything you do – your movement, your thoughts, and your memory. Often it does not act directly. Instead it may control tiny amounts of chemicals in the blood which in turn have a strong effect on another part of the body.

Although it looks quite simple, the brain is immensely complicated. It is a mass of whitish tissue, quite soft to the touch. The brain takes up about half the volume of the head. It is positioned at the top of the head, above the eyes and ears, extending lower down at the back of the head.

Almost as important as your brain is the rest of the nervous system. The **spinal cord** runs from the brain down the spine. The brain and spinal cord together make up the **central nervous system.**

Along the length of the spinal cord thread-like **nerves** branch off, dividing and connecting with almost every part of the body. Nerves carry messages from the sense organs to the brain. They also carry instructions from the brain to other parts of the body.

The brain works like a complicated but compact telephone network, with a bewildering flow of messages passing through, being sorted, and directed to their proper destination.

The brain and its spinal cord are kept in contact with every part of the body by a finely branched system of nerves through which tiny electrical signals are continually passing.

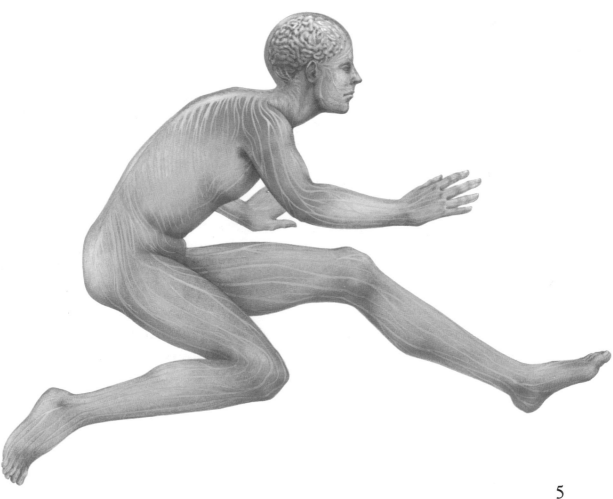

The brain's protective coverings

Because the brain is so important, it needs very good protection from accidents.

Humans stand upright, keeping the head and brain well away from bumps and knocks. Even so, much more reliable protection is needed, and the brain is protected inside the skull, which is made of tough bone.

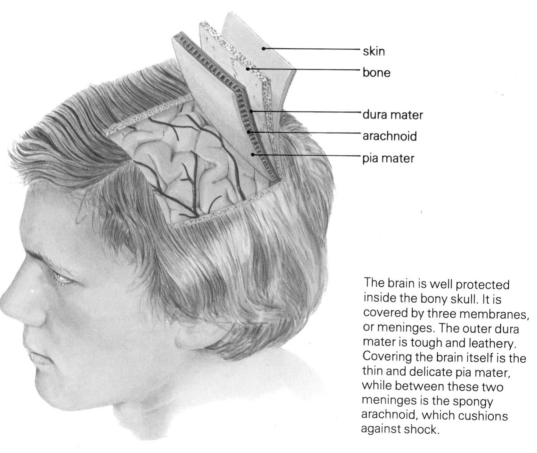

- skin
- bone
- dura mater
- arachnoid
- pia mater

The brain is well protected inside the bony skull. It is covered by three membranes, or meninges. The outer dura mater is tough and leathery. Covering the brain itself is the thin and delicate pia mater, while between these two meninges is the spongy arachnoid, which cushions against shock.

Although the skull is thin, it is extremely strong because of its round shape. A rigid ball is one of the strongest shapes known. An egg, for example, is very strong, considering how thin its shell is.

So the soft and delicate brain is protected and supported by the tough skull against direct damage from outside. However even though the skull is strong and rigid, a heavy blow could still shake the brain, and cause damage. Further protection is needed, and is provided by three layers of skin-like **membranes**, called the **meninges**, which completely cover the brain. The outer membrane is called the dura mater (a Latin word, like many of the names for parts of the body). This layer is tough and leathery, and provides good protection and support.

Closest to the brain is another layer called the pia mater. It is much thinner, closely following every bump and wrinkle on the brain's surface. Between the two is the spongy arachnoid. Its spaces are filled with liquid, in which the whole brain floats, providing the final layer of protection.

There are also large spaces within the brain, and these too are filled with the same liquid, so the brain's soft tissue will not shift about as we move our heads.

The spinal cord

The spinal cord is an extension of the brain, extending about two-thirds of the way down the middle of the back to just below the ribs.

It is a rod of brain tissue, with a small hole running through it. The whole cord is covered with membranes, just like the brain, and it too is bathed inside and out with protective fluid.

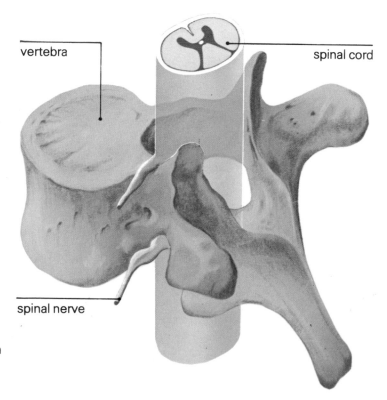

vertebra

spinal cord

spinal nerve

The delicate spinal cord is protected by the vertebrae. Each vertebra has a bony arch surrounding the spinal cord.

8

Like the brain, the spinal cord needs protection. While the brain is safely enclosed in a rigid skull, the spinal cord is surrounded by a set of bones called vertebrae. These make up the spinal column, which must be able to flex as we bend and turn. At the same time, the spinal column has to be strong enough to support the weight of the body, and to give very secure protection to the spinal cord.

It might seem that flexibility, strength and the protection of its fragile contents could not all be achieved by the spinal column, but its ingenious construction makes all these possible.

The spinal column is made up of more than two dozen ring-shaped vertebrae. The spinal cord runs through the hole in each vertebra, and is completely protected by an arch of bone. Bony outgrowths of the vertebrae interlock, so each vertebra can only move a small amount. This is not sufficient to pinch or damage the spinal cord.

Between each pair of vertebrae are small gaps through which nerves can pass, branching off from the spinal cord itself. The whole complicated structure is held tightly together by tough straps of ligament, and by powerful muscles.

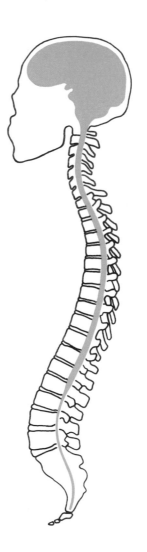

The central nervous system is made up of the brain and spinal cord, all protected within the rigid skull and flexible spine.

9

The structure of the brain

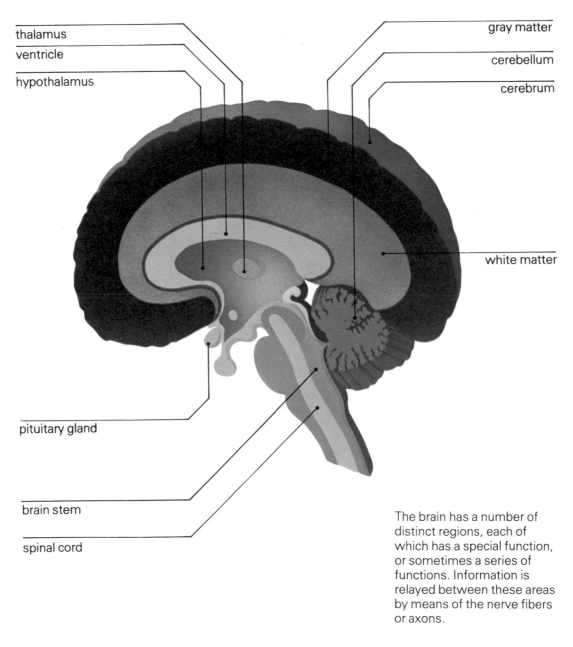

thalamus

ventricle

hypothalamus

gray matter

cerebellum

cerebrum

white matter

pituitary gland

brain stem

spinal cord

The brain has a number of distinct regions, each of which has a special function, or sometimes a series of functions. Information is relayed between these areas by means of the nerve fibers or axons.

The brain looks rather like a large pale pink walnut kernel. Its surface is deeply folded and wrinkled, and the upper part is divided almost into two by a very deep groove.

This wrinkled surface layer is the largest part of the brain, and is called the **cerebrum**. In most other animals the cerebrum is quite small, but in man it has grown so large that it covers almost all of the rest of the brain.

The cerebrum, together with other parts of the brain, grows out of the **brain stem**, which is a swelling at the top of the spinal cord.

A little further down the brain stem is the **cerebellum**, which is about one-eighth the size of the cerebrum, but outwardly similar in appearance. It is even more wrinkled, and is positioned right at the back of the head.

Several smaller parts of the brain also grow out from the brain stem – the **thalamus** and **hypothalamus**. These are completely covered by the bulk of the cerebrum.

A series of large spaces, or **ventricles**, runs through the whole brain structure, and these are filled with liquid.

The brain stem

The brain stem is sometimes called the oldest part of the brain, because it is the main part of the brain in most primitive animals. It controls most of the important functions of the body, and is our life support system. If the brain stem is not damaged, it is actually possible for the body to remain alive for some time after the rest of the brain has been destroyed in an accident.

The brain stem acts with the spinal cord to control such vital functions as the regular beating of the heart, blood pressure and breathing.

Most important of all, the brain stem controls consciousness, switching activity of the brain off as we sleep and on again as we wake. Even as we sleep, the brain stem monitors and checks our vital functions, keeping the body running smoothly.

The brain stem works like a computer, continuously checking and monitoring the information coming into the brain via the nervous system. Then it acts on this information, sending out messages into the nervous system to control the whole body. We are not aware of all this activity, although we may notice its effects. The brain stem controls functions like breathing quite automatically.

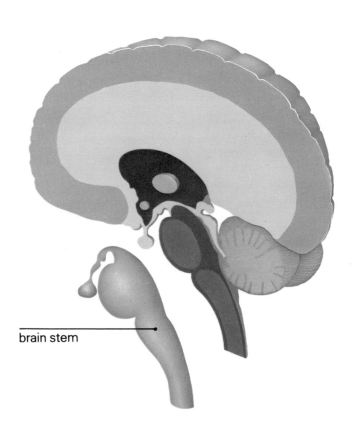

brain stem

control center

perspiration

growth

breathing

temperature

blood pressure

sleep

The brain stem, lying beneath the brain, is the body's life-support system. It works automatically, without our being aware of its function, to maintain the processes essential for life.

13

The cerebrum

The cerebrum is probably the youngest part of the brain, or at least the most recently developed in the course of evolution. In man it is so big that it covers almost all the rest of the brain, and makes up about seventy per cent of its whole volume.

The cerebrum consists of two large domes, or **hemispheres**, of brain tissue, joined together by a bridge called the **corpus callosum**, at the bottom of a deep cleft.

Nerve cells are packed in the gray matter covering the cerebrum. To allow the maximum possible number of nerve cells, the cerebral surface is crumpled like a sheet of screwed-up paper.

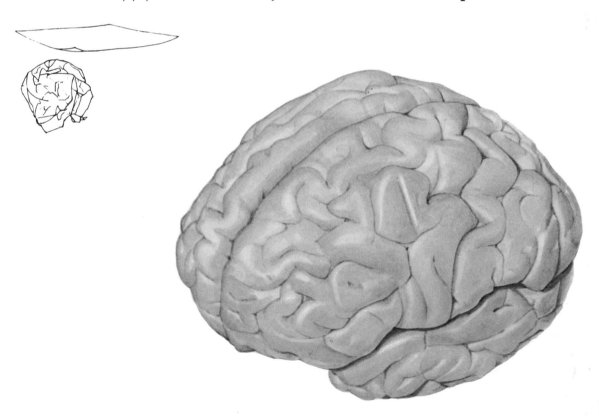

14

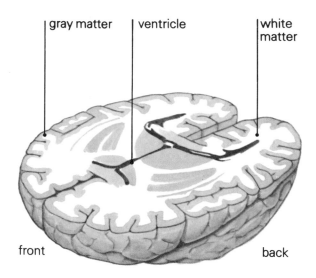

gray matter | ventricle | white matter

front   back

There are two quite different layers in the hemispheres making up the cerebrum. On the outside is a thin layer called the **cortex**, or **gray matter**, which completely covers the cerebrum. The rest of the cerebrum is made of **white matter** – the same soft tissue which makes up most of the brain.

Tiny nerve cells are closely packed in the thin layer of cortex or gray matter. The nerve fibers carrying messages down into the brain are found in the white matter. The folding of the surface of the brain means that there is more area of cortex, and therefore more brain cells can be packed in.

The cerebrum is responsible for our intelligence and for most of our skills. Here the information received from sense organs is examined and acted upon. It is the activity of our comparatively large and efficient cerebrum which makes the brain of man so much more efficient than that of other animals.

Gray matter covers the outside surface of the cerebrum. Inside, the greatest volume of the brain is made up from nerve fibers or axons, and this is called the white matter.

The cerebellum

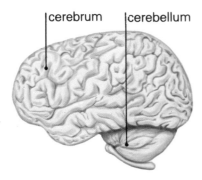

side view

cerebrum   cerebellum

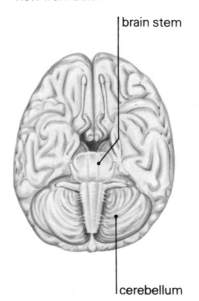

view from below

brain stem

cerebellum

The cerebellum is positioned at the back of the brain, behind the cerebrum. It makes up about ten per cent of the brain's volume. Like the cerebrum, it also has an outer layer of gray matter, the rest being made up of white matter.

The inner structure of the cerebellum is quite unlike that of the rest of the brain, as the tiny cells in its cortex are arranged with almost mathematical precision. The cells are positioned in such regular order that scientists have been able to work out their connections, which resemble an enormous electrical wiring diagram.

The cerebellum works in a unique way. The rest of the brain produces signals which cause other parts of the nervous system to react. But the function of the cerebellum is to reduce or stop some of these signals, and so it controls coordination and balance.

The signals processed by the cerebellum are instructions for muscular movement that have come from the cerebrum. The signals are very strong, and if they were not adjusted in the cerebellum, we would not be able to make any accurate or delicate movements. We would be unable to pick up a glass of water without spilling it, or to walk without staggering.

16

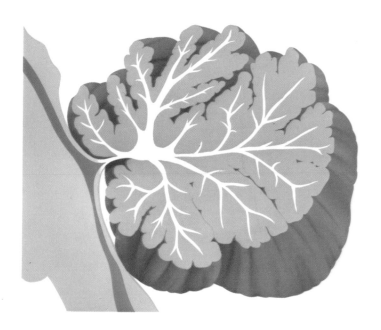

The cerebellum is a small outgrowth from the brain stem. It is very deeply folded and creased, and has a complicated but regular structure in which its neurons are arranged.

Coordination and physical skills are under the control of the cerebellum, which processes nerve impulses passing in the muscles. Without the cerebellum, the gymnast, athlete and musician would not have the fine muscular control they need.

17

The neurons

Nerve cells or neurons carry nerve impulses about the body. Although there are several different types, they are built on a similar plan, with a large cell body and a long axon to carry the impulse.

The tiny nerve cells that make up the brain and the rest of the nervous system are called **neurons**. There are 12 billion in the brain alone, and many million more in the nerves. Even this huge number makes up only a small part of the brain. Packed tightly around and between the neurons is another type of cell called **glial cells**. Their purpose is to provide a supporting framework for the neurons.

The neuron carries messages by means of a long strand or thread called an **axon**. The axon grows from the neuron's rounded cell body, where the other functions of the cell take place.

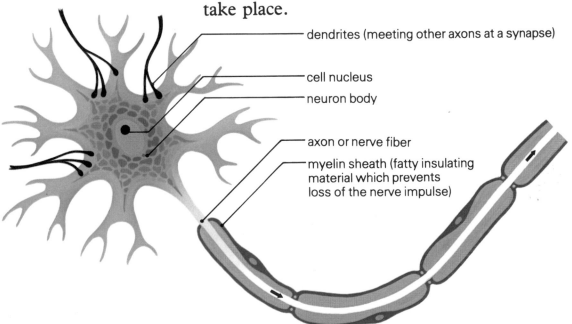

dendrites (meeting other axons at a synapse)

cell nucleus

neuron body

axon or nerve fiber

myelin sheath (fatty insulating material which prevents loss of the nerve impulse)

Nerve ending in a muscle fiber.
When a nerve impulse is
received here,
the muscle fiber will contract.

Many other fine threads called **dendrites** also branch out from the neuron's cell body. The axon is longest of all – sometimes 3 ft (90 cm) or more in length, although the cell body is so tiny that it can only be seen under the most powerful microscopes. Signals are passed along the axon, from one cell to the next. They pass across where the branching end of an axon meets the dendrites of another cell, at a junction called a **synapse**.

The neuron can only pass the simplest information – either "on" or "off." All our mental activities are based on this simple "on-off" signal, but when enough neurons are involved, very complicated information can be handled in a code rather like the special simplified languages used to "talk" with computers.

How messages are passed along a neuron

A signal carried by a neuron may seem like an electrical current carried along a wire, but in reality it is quite different. A tiny electrical charge *is* produced, but the movement of the signal along the axon is more like a burning gunpowder fuse. It moves along at anything between 5 and 300 ft (1·5–90 m) each second.

The axon is a thin tube filled with chemicals dissolved in water. Many are covered on the outside with a layer of fatty material, like electrical insulation.

Passing a signal along an axon involves movement of **ions**, or tiny electrically charged particles of two common metallic elements – sodium and potassium. Normally there is more potassium inside the axon and more sodium outside.

When a signal is passed, the thin skin or membrane covering the axon changes to allow the ions to leak through, causing a sudden change in the electrical properties at that point. These changes surge along the axon like a wave.

When the signal reaches the synapse, it must cross a small gap to reach the next neuron. Tiny bubbles in the knobs at the end of the axon contain chemical substances called **transmitters**. They are released as the signal reaches them, and they flow across the gap in the synapse. When they contact the dendrites of the next cell, they start the movement of sodium and potassium, passing on the signal.

Now the first neuron returns to its normal resting state, waiting for another signal.

At the synapse, or connection between two neurons, nerve impulses are carried across a tiny gap by means of chemical transmitters. These fire off another nerve impulse in the next neuron, passing on the message. In this way information is passed around the whole nervous system.

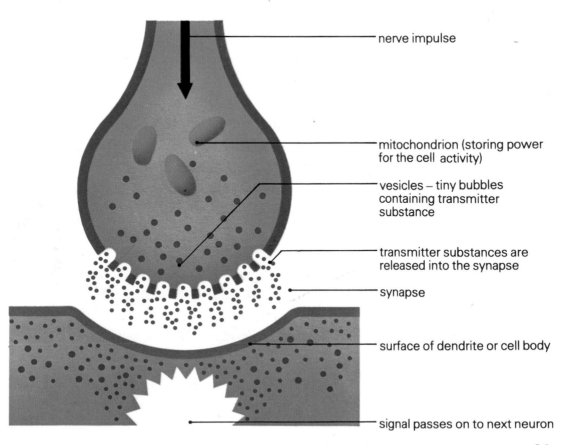

nerve impulse

mitochondrion (storing power for the cell activity)

vesicles – tiny bubbles containing transmitter substance

transmitter substances are released into the synapse

synapse

surface of dendrite or cell body

signal passes on to next neuron

The chemical transmitters which carry a signal across the gap of the synapse can be of two different types.

Some are called **excitatory chemicals**. These are the substances which pass on a message to the next neuron. This, in turn, begins the electrical changes which will cause signals to be produced and passed along its axon.

The other transmitters are called **inhibitory chemicals**. Their function is to prevent a signal being produced in another neuron.

Thousands of neurons are in contact with each other through synapses, and many will be producing excitatory or inhibitory signals. The neuron will not produce a signal unless it receives more excitatory (or "on") messages than inhibitory (or "off") messages.

A signal from one or two neurons is not enough to trigger off another – it must receive several signals at once. This means that any occasional accidental signals from the thousands of neurons around it will not cause a false message to be passed. It is rather like the principle of voting, where the neuron needs the "votes" of a number of other neurons before it is able to signal.

A nerve impulse or signal is not simply passed from one neuron to the next. It needs several nerve impulses to fire off another neuron and transmit the signal onward. As the signal is passed toward a muscle, for example, it must involve fewer and fewer neurons until, as in the drawing below, four separate signals stimulate a nerve impulse in the last neuron. This then passes its message to the muscle fiber.

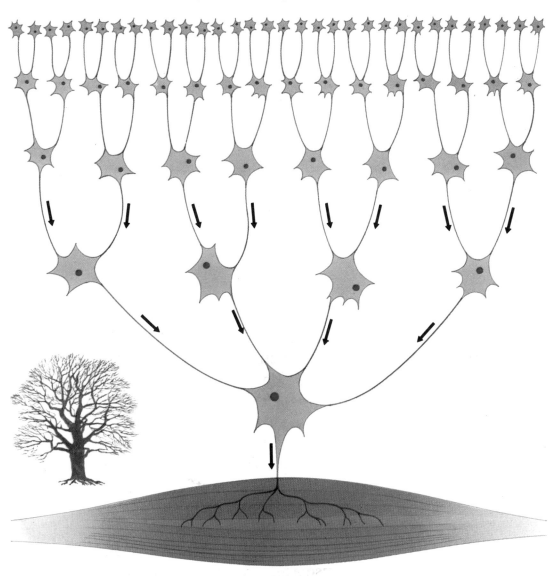

In the nervous "tree" fine branches join and eventually pass a signal through the "trunk" – a single nerve fiber.

Measuring brain waves

All over the brain, all the time, our neurons are passing their electrical signals. These flicker across the surface of the brain, spreading out like ripples from a stone dropped into a pool. If these tiny electrical signals were lights, the whole brain would twinkle endlessly, even during sleep.

Though tiny, the electrical signals from the brain can be measured, even through the skull and skin, with the aid of a special machine. Wires are stuck on to the skin, and these pick up the signals, carrying them to the machine. This records the electrical currents generated in the brain cells in graph form on a moving strip of paper. This graph is called an electroencephalogram – **EEG** for short.

An EEG shows that electrical signals are not produced steadily by the brain. Instead they come in regular short bursts. These produce a pattern on the EEG like a series of waves, sometimes called "brain waves."

The electrical activity of the brain is produced in a series of pulses which can be measured and recorded on a moving paper trace as a zigzag line. This line, or EEG, shows the amount of activity produced by the brain.

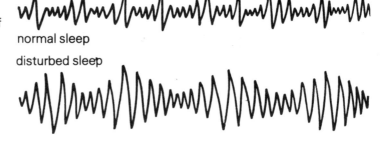

normal sleep

disturbed sleep

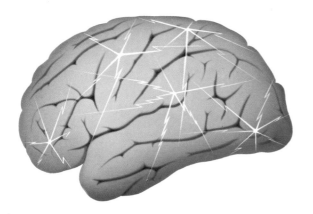

As nerve impulses pass through the brain, electrical signals spread across the surface like ripples. The brain continuously produces these electrical signals.

Brain waves show that the brain is always active, even when we sleep. The sleeping brain produces large slow waves. When we are awake, but relaxed, brain waves are faster and smaller. Activity or deep thought causes sharp jagged waves.

During brain operations it is possible to measure brain electricity much more accurately. Doctors have learned the exact function of some parts of the brain by measuring the electricity produced on its surface when, for example, a finger is pricked, or a leg is moved. The measurements have been used to produce "maps" of the cortex.

The electroencephalograph measures the electrical activity of the brain by means of sensors which are attached to the skin.

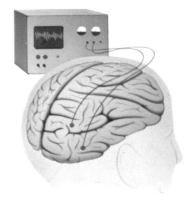

25

Routes through the
nervous system

The electrical activity of the neurons does not take place only in the brain. From the top of the head to the tips of the toes, nerves spread through the body. They are bundles of axons, or nerve fibers, dividing and becoming finer the further away they are from the brain and spinal cord.

The neurons' cell bodies are grouped in the gray matter on the brain's surface, in similar gray matter inside the spinal cord, and in small lumps called **ganglia**, near the spine.

Through the nervous system, messages pass *to* the brain from the sense organs in the eyes, ears and mouth, as well as from the organs of touch over the whole surface of the body, and even in some internal organs. The neurons that carry these messages are called sensory neurons. More signals pass *from* the brain and spinal cord, back around the body, carried by motor neurons.

Signals pass along the whole system very quickly, but not nearly as fast as in a normal electrical circuit. It takes a certain amount of time for the signals to be carried across the synapses by the transmitter chemicals. For this reason the nerve axons are immensely long so that the messages can be carried as fast as possible without being delayed by unnecessary synapses.

The brain is involved in many of our simple daily activities. This person is testing the temperature of a bowl of water. When the foot is dipped into the water, sense organs in the skin are stimulated by the temperature and produce a signal. This is passed along nerve fibers to the brain, eventually reaching the cortex. The brain examines the incoming signals and assesses the temperature. If this is not too hot or too cold, the brain produces more signals, which pass back down the spine to leg muscles which lower the foot into the water.

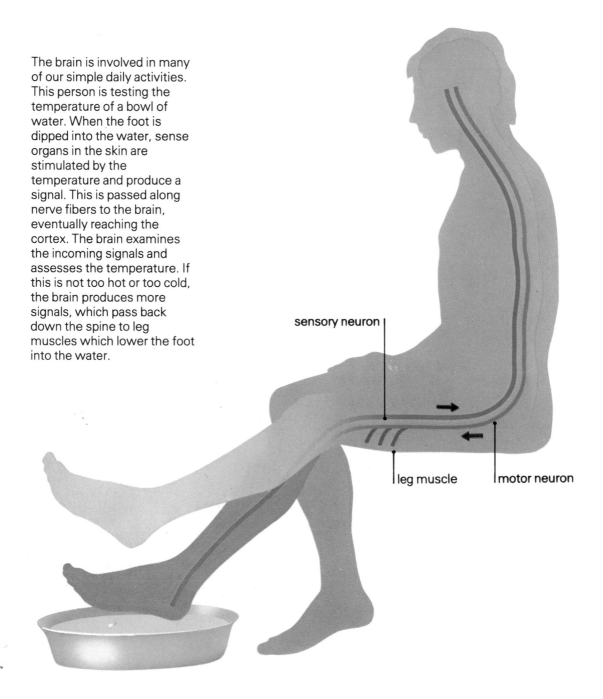

sensory neuron

leg muscle

motor neuron

The neuron network

It is difficult to realize exactly how complicated the connections of nerve cells can be. The branching ends of an axon not only touch the nearest cell, but can be in contact with another 50,000 cells or even more.

We know that messages pass from one neuron to the next in the network of cells, and a repeated signal usually always passes along the same path. If we want to say the word "brain," instructions for speech pass through the brain along a special series of pathways. If we want to say "brain" in a deeper or higher tone of voice, the muscles of the voice box must be instructed to move in another way, so the messages must move in different pathways.

The brain can select different sets of pathways to get similar results. Because of this ability, people can often overcome brain injuries, learning to use different parts of the brain to duplicate the functions of the damaged parts.

This is important to us because, unlike other body cells, brain cells cannot grow or repair themselves after we are born. Brain cells are dying every minute, but we have so many remaining to take over their function that we do not usually notice any ill effects.

Part of a circuit board used in a computer. Connections in the brain are very much more complicated, so the brain can handle more information than any machine.

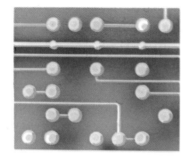

28

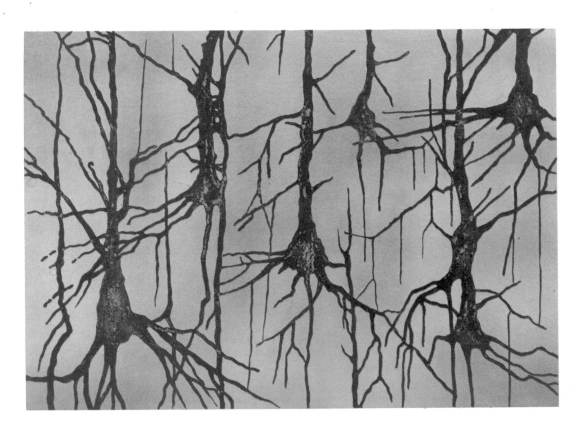

This drawing is made from an
actual photomicrograph of
part of the brain. It shows
how the neurons are arranged
in a regular manner, with
many interconnections
between nearby neurons.
There are many finer
connections, too small and
too complicated to be shown
here.

29

Reflex action

Control by the brain is essential for many of our functions, but in some situations it is necessary for the body to react very fast indeed, without waiting for instructions. These emergency reactions are called **reflexes.**

Jumping away from a pin-prick is a very common reaction which prevents the body from harm. It takes place very quickly, before we even recognize what has happened. This is a reflex at work.

Tiny sense organs called **receptors**, in the skin, register the pin-prick. They immediately pass signals into nerves running up the arm toward the spinal cord. The signals are then conveyed to other nerve fibers (neurons) which carry them deep into the gray matter inside the spinal cord.

When the finger is pricked, a message passes rapidly to the spinal cord. Here further impulses are generated and passed to the brain and to the muscles.

Before the message has reached the brain, muscles have been instructed to jerk the arm away from the pin. We are only conscious of the pain *after* the arm has been moved to safety.

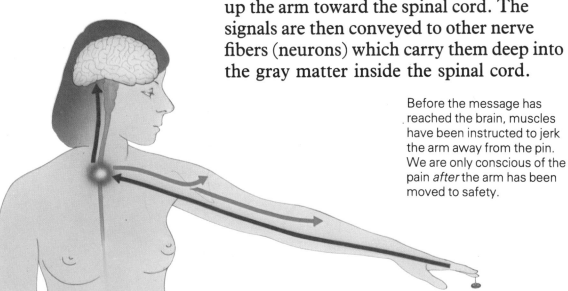

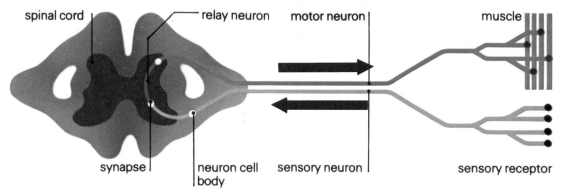

spinal cord | relay neuron | motor neuron | muscle

synapse | neuron cell body | sensory neuron | sensory receptor

Here the signals move off in two directions. Some contact nerve fibers leading directly back into the arm muscles. They cause the arm muscles to pull violently, jerking the whole arm away from the pinprick. Part of the original signal is still speeding up the spinal cord to the brain.

A split second later we realize we have been pricked. It hurts! The brain now instructs the head and eyes to move and inspect the injury.

Sometimes we have to put up with a pinprick, as for example when we receive a vaccination. However, we know about this in advance, and although the prick of the hypodermic needle starts the reflex, the brain has already sent an *inhibitory* message down the spinal cord. There the reflex is stopped from being completed. The arm, therefore, will not jump away.

This cross-section of the spine shows how nerve impulses enter and leave the spinal cord. In a reflex action impulses pass directly from the sensory neuron to the motor neuron, along a short relay neuron inside the spinal cord.

The autonomic nervous system

Some of the activities of the nervous system, like thinking and the control of movement, are very obvious to us. But the nervous system is also working without our realizing it, controlling our internal organs.

This is the responsibility of a special part of the nervous system called the **autonomic nervous system**. It regulates our blood circulation, digestion, breathing, reproductive organs and the elimination of waste from the body. It also controls important glands which have a powerful effect on the body. The autonomic nervous system works independently of most of the brain and its cell bodies are grouped in ganglia near the spine. It operates entirely by reflexes, and although the brain stem is also involved in its activity, we are not consciously aware of this.

The system is actually split into two parts, called the **sympathetic** and **parasympathetic nervous systems**. They work against each other. One system will stimulate an organ, such as a gland, making it work harder. The other system stops it from working. First one takes over, then the other, and the result is that the organ is kept working at just the right level.

The sympathetic nervous system can be

seen working when we are angry or frightened. Its action makes the heart beat faster and lets us breathe more deeply. The pupils of the eye become larger, and we go pale as blood drains from the skin to feed muscles we might need for "fight or flight." This has all happened because the sympathetic system has taken over, to make the body ready for an emergency.

Most of our normal body functions are controlled by the parasympathetic nervous system. When we are angry or excited, the sympathetic nervous system takes over, increasing the rate at which the heart beats, and making us breathe deeply to take in more oxygen.

The functions of the cortex

Different areas of the brain are responsible for registering the sense of touch, and for controlling body movement. The position of these areas can be "mapped" on the surface of the cortex.

Muscles in our internal organs work automatically, but most of our muscles work only when we wish to move them. These are voluntary muscles.

Voluntary movements, such as walking, moving the arms, and using the fingers, are directly controlled by the brain. A narrow strip of cortex across the top of the cerebrum is called the **motor cortex**, and it is concerned with organizing our movement.

The motor cortex collects information from other parts of the brain, including signals from sense organs. When a decision

The motor cortex
The areas of the cortex used to control movement are similar to those registering the senses, with the face and hands being especially important.

swallowing

tongue, jaw

lips

face
eye, brow

neck

fingers, hand

wrist

shoulder, arm

trunk
hip, knee
ankle
toes

34

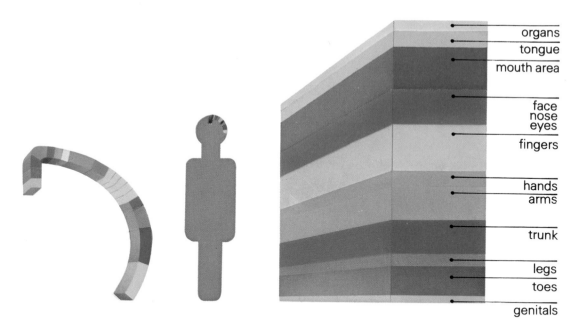

organs
tongue
mouth area
face
nose
eyes
fingers
hands
arms
trunk
legs
toes
genitals

has been made to move a muscle, or a whole series of muscles, it issues its instructions to the proper part of the body.

Different parts of the motor cortex have special functions, each controlling movement in a certain part of the body. Important and complex parts, such as the hands and lips, require very careful control, and the many neurons needed for this work take up large areas of the cortex. Less complicated parts need less control, so smaller areas of the cortex are responsible for them.

In the same way that movement is controlled by the motor cortex, special parts of the **sensory cortex** are responsible for touch. Other parts look after vision, hearing, and all our other senses.

The sensory cortex
The relative importance of different senses can be seen by measuring the area they take up on the surface of the cortex. The large area taken up by hands, face and eyes can be clearly seen.

35

Where thinking takes place

Movement and the senses take up only two narrow strips across the cortex of the cerebrum.

The rest of the cortex does not have such easily recognized purposes. It contains the association areas, and is probably the part of the brain where "thinking" takes place. By thinking, we mean examining and interpreting the huge number of signals coming into the brain, and deciding on any action to take – or sometimes deciding *not* to act.

Some functions, among them speech, are dotted about the cortex in small patches. Speech is also controlled by several different areas of the brain, as well as by a part of the cortex.

The way the association areas work is not well understood. Sometimes quite large parts of the brain can be damaged, by disease or injury, without having much effect. On the other hand, damage to small parts of the brain can sometimes have very serious effect. The way the brain works is much more complicated than it at first appears.

Very large parts of the brain have no obvious purpose at all, but as the neurons are interconnected in such a complicated way, it is believed that all of the brain must have some function. Perhaps some of this "spare" brain comes into use to replace neurons that die as we get older.

As we view objects, images formed on the retina of the eye produce nerve impulses. These are carried to the brain, eventually arriving at the visual cortex, a narrow band across the cerebrum. Some of this information passes to the association areas of the cortex, where a choice is made. In this picture the boy is choosing between two drinks. The motor area of the cortex then produces signals which are sent to the arm and hand muscles, to cause the desired action.

The "logical" brain

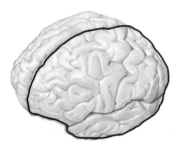

The cerebrum is divided almost into two sections by a deep groove. In some serious brain operations it has been necessary to divide them completely. When this was done, surgeons found that each half could work on its own, as a separate "brain," but the right and left sections are very different in the way they work.

Each side of the brain controls the *opposite* side of the body, nerve fibers crossing over in the corpus callosum at the bottom of the groove between the hemispheres.

Normally both sides of the brain must work together, and they communicate with each other through the corpus callosum. When this is cut, and the two sections are kept apart, the differences between them can be seen.

In most people the left side of the brain is responsible for "logical" thinking. This is the careful, step-by-step reasoning which we need for say, mathematics. We also use the left side to control our speech, an immensely complicated process which no machine has been able to master. Separate small pieces of the left cerebrum look after the actions needed for writing, for the sounds we produce as we speak, and for the naming of things we can see.

Sometimes an old person has a stroke, which damages this part of the brain, and he or she may then not be able to speak properly.

The left side of the brain works in this way in most people, but in left-handed people the right side of the brain may be the "logical" half. In some left-handed people speech may be controlled by *both* sides.

The left side of the brain is where logical or calculatory thinking takes place. While working out a problem such as arithmetic or a chess game, the left side of the brain is intensely active.

The "artistic" brain

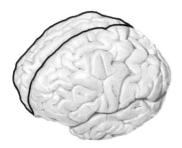

The right side of the brain is the "artistic" part. It is concerned with understanding and interpreting the world about us – but not usually with speech.

The right side of the brain looks at situations and problems in general, and gives us an immediate answer or a solution. This is quite different from the way the left side works, in a series of deliberate, careful steps.

The "artistic" brain is concerned with looking at our surroundings. It can, for example, pick out a familiar face from a crowd of people, but the left side of the brain then has to supply that person's name from the memory.

Musical abilities also depend on the right side of the brain, together with visual skills such as painting.

Art and music are both functions for which we use the right side of the brain.

Although each half of the brain can operate on its own, both sections must work together if we are to function normally. For most activities we use both sides together. Imagine that you are writing a description of a picture. First you look at the picture, and the right side of your brain becomes active. A scientist could prove this by using an EEG. Now you start to write, and the left side of the brain takes over. When you look at a complicated diagram, both the "logical" and "artistic" parts of the brain are needed. Both sides work smoothly together.

The right side of the brain is used for "creative" thinking, often involving a visual problem or puzzle. The right side of the brain is skillful in recognizing shapes and patterns.

41

Learning and memory

The picture on the left shows part of the brain of a child of 3 months. The picture on the right shows the same part of the brain at 24 months. In the immature brain there are not many connections between the neurons. As the brain develops, and we add experiences to our memory store, the connections between the neurons become much more complicated.

Learning means making a tiny change in the structure of the brain. Signals find their way through the network of neurons in the brain, and repeated signals tend to take the same pathway each time. These pathways are made between neurons by way of synapses.

If we were to begin some new activity, such as learning to play a guitar, signals would have to be transmitted through already existing pathways to give the proper

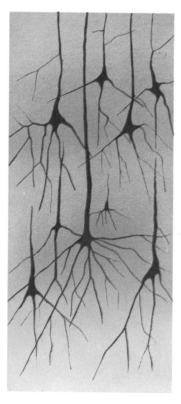

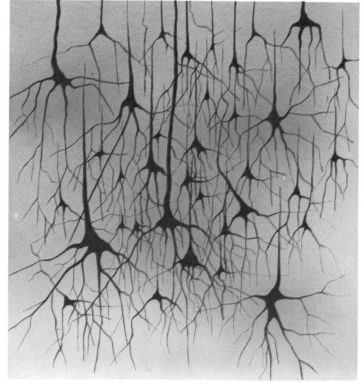

instruction to the fingers to press the guitar strings in a particular way. Since there are at first only a few pathways to choose from, the finger movements would be rather clumsy.

With more practice, the same message is passed more and more often, and the pathways begin to change. More synapses develop for the instructions to the finger muscles. As these new pathways develop, we find it much easier to move the fingers exactly as required, and eventually can play well without even looking at what we are doing. A whole section of brain has been "rewired" to act as a music-playing computer.

The brain of a young baby has far fewer connections between its neurons than an adult. These connections increase very quickly as the baby learns about its surroundings. This is why it is important to talk to very young babies and give them plenty of toys to catch their interest while their brains develop more fully.

Learning and memory are similar, and both probably depend on alterations in the brain. Memory is not well understood, but it may also depend on changes in the pathways taken through the brain by signals produced by neurons. Some scientists also think that special chemicals may be involved in storing memories. Memory is not based on any special part of the brain, but is stored over large parts of its surface.

There are several different types of memory. One is very short, and consists of a quick scan through all the material received from the sense organs. Nearly all is quickly forgotten. Sometimes something crops up which interests us, so we think about it for a while. It too will disappear within a few seconds, unless we repeat it to ourselves several times, or "rehearse" it. This seems to make the memory "stick" in the mind. It is what we have to do to remember a telephone number. After we have rehearsed it several times, or have used the number frequently, it becomes a permanent memory.

Once something is filed away in our memory, it is there for good. We sometimes "forget" something, but what really happens is that we forget how to find it in the vast storage system of the brain. Probably the proper pathway is no longer effective, because it has not been used enough. The fact we are seeking remains filed away until we can get at it along another pathway through the brain. It can also be truly lost in old age if enough brain cells die so that the storage area no longer works.

Information stored in our memory is sometimes easily accessible, but can be "mislaid" in the whole enormous filing system. There is always a large amount of unused storage space in the memory.

Glossary

Autonomic nervous system: the part of the nervous system which functions without our conscious awareness. It controls all of the life-support systems of the body.

Axon: long thread, extending from the body of a neuron, along which a signal is carried.

Brain stem: bulge at the top of the spinal cord, forming the bottom part of the brain. The brain stem controls most of our vital functions, and is a major part of the autonomic nervous system.

Central nervous system: the brain and spinal cord are the most essential parts of the nervous system, together making up the central nervous system.

Cerebellum: small and deeply folded area at the back of the brain, concerned with controlling coordination of movement and balance.

Cerebrum: large domed area making up the largest part of the brain. Our reasoning, memory and senses are controlled in the cerebrum.

Corpus callosum: small strip of tissue connecting the two hemispheres of the cerebrum. Signals passed between the right and left hemispheres cross the corpus callosum.

Cortex: the outer layer of the cerebrum, made up from gray matter.

Dendrites: the finely branched endings of an axon, which are in contact with another neuron at the synapse.

EEG: electroencephalogram; a measurement of the electrical activity within the brain, recorded as a graph on a strip of moving paper.

Excitatory chemicals: transmitter substances, present in tiny amounts, which stimulate a neuron to produce a signal.

Ganglia: small groups of neurons, in which nerve signals are processed.

Glial cells: special cells which are packed around and between the neurons. They help support the delicate nervous tissue.

Gray matter: part of the nerve tissue in which the bodies of the neurons are situated. Mostly on the *outside* of the brain, and the *inside* of the spinal cord.

Hemispheres: the two dome-like structures which make up most of the cerebrum.

Hypothalamus: small part of the brain which is concerned with expressing emotion (such as changes in pulse rate, sweating, etc.), controlling sleep, and governing the action of the most important gland in the body, the pituitary.

Inhibitory chemicals: transmitter substances which prevent the production of a signal in a neuron.

Ion: an electrically charged chemical particle. When common salt, or sodium chloride, is dissolved in water, it splits into two separate ions: sodium and chloride.

Membrane: a thin covering to a cell or tissue. Neurons are covered by a very thin membrane, through which transmitter chemicals pass.

Meninges: skin-like coverings over the brain and part of the spinal cord. There are three layers: the dura mater, arachnoid and pia mater.

Motor cortex: part of the surface of the cerebrum in which instructions for muscle movement are processed.

Nerve: bundle of axons, through which signals are passed to and from the brain.

Neuron: nerve cell, which passes signals to other neurons along a thread-like axon.

Parasympathetic nervous system: part of the autonomic nervous system which influences the pupil of the eye, pulse rate, breathing, the digestion, and sexual organs. Its action is, in general, opposite to that of the sympathetic nervous system.

Receptors: groups of cells which can receive a signal, and pass it on to the nervous system. Typical receptors are those registering touch, in the skin, and light, in the retina of the eye.

Reflex: an automatic response of the body, which initially does not involve the brain. An example of a reflex is jerking the hand away from a hot object.

Sensory cortex: part of the surface of the cerebrum in which information from the sense organs is processed and converted into the "sensations" that we feel.

Spinal cord: very large bundle of nerve cells running down from the brain inside the spine.

Sympathetic nervous system: part of the autonomic nervous system influencing pulse rate, breathing, and many other functions. Its actions are generally opposite to those of the parasympathetic nervous system, preparing the body for action in an emergency. It also controls speech and swallowing.

Synapse: the gap between a neuron and the dendrites of another neuron.

Thalamus: part of the brain which processes information from the sense organs, and provides some control over muscle activity.

Transmitter substances: chemicals present in tiny amounts, which carry a signal across a synapse, between the neurons.

Ventricles: fluid-filled spaces inside the brain, also running down the middle of the spinal cord.

White matter: masses of closely packed axons. White matter makes up most of the *interior* of the brain, and the *outside* of the spinal cord.

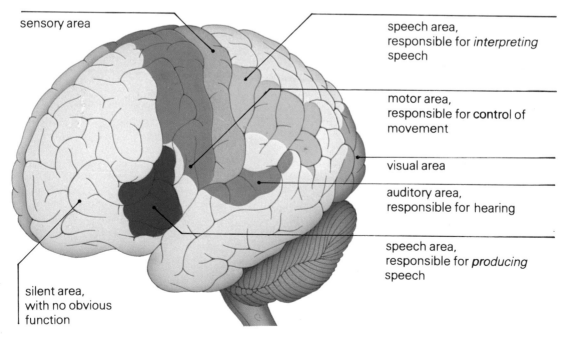

sensory area

speech area, responsible for *interpreting* speech

motor area, responsible for **control** of movement

visual area

auditory area, responsible for hearing

speech area, responsible for *producing* speech

silent area, with no obvious function

47

Index

48

Printed in Great Britain by Cambus Litho, East Kilbride, Scotland

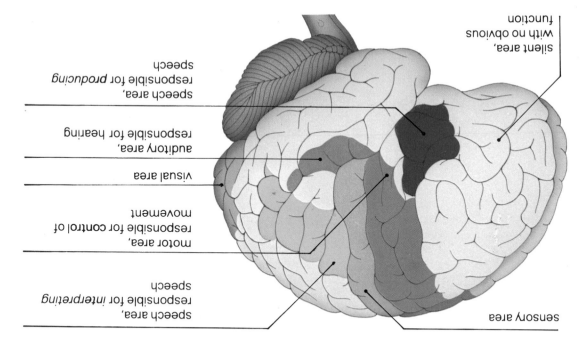

silent area, with no obvious function

speech area, responsible for *producing* speech

auditory area, responsible for hearing

visual area

motor area, responsible for control of movement

speech area, responsible for *interpreting* speech

sensory area

Receptors: groups of cells which can receive a signal, and pass it on to the nervous system. Typical receptors are those registering touch, in the skin, and light, in the retina of the eye.

Reflex: an automatic response of the body, which initially does not involve the brain. An example of a reflex is jerking the hand away from a hot object.

Sensory cortex: part of the surface of the cerebrum in which information from the sense organs is processed and conveyed into the "sensations" that we feel.

Sympathetic nervous system: part of the autonomic nervous system influencing pulse rate, breathing, and many other functions. Its actions are generally opposite to those of the parasympathetic nervous system, preparing the body for action in an emergency. It also controls speech and swallowing.

Synapse: the gap between a neuron and the dendrites of another neuron.

Spinal cord: very large bundle of nerve cells running down from the brain inside the spine.

Thalamus: part of the brain which processes information from the sense organs, and provides some control over muscle activity.

Transmitter substances: chemicals present in tiny amounts, which carry a signal across a synapse, between the neurons.

Ventricles: fluid-filled spaces inside the brain, also running down the middle of the spinal cord.

White matter: masses of closely packed axons. White matter makes up most of the *interior* of the brain, and the *outside* of the spinal cord.

Index

Printed in Great Britain by Cambus Litho, East Kilbride, Scotland

COMBATING
TERRORISM

//////////////////

By J.M. Bedell

Content Adviser: Jarret Brachman, Ph.D., author of *Global Jihadism: Theory and Practice*
and senior U.S. government counterterrorism consultant

Reading Adviser: Alexa L. Sandmann, Ed.D., Professor of Literacy,
College and Graduate School of Education, Health, and Human Services,
Kent State University

COMPASS POINT BOOKS
a capstone imprint

Compass Point Books
151 Good Counsel Drive
P.O. Box 669
Mankato, MN 56002-0669

 This book was manufactured with paper containing
at least 10 percent post-consumer waste.

Editor: Brenda Haugen
Designer: Heidi Thompson
Media Researcher: Eric Gohl
Library Consultant: Kathleen Baxter
Production Specialist: Jane Klenk

Image Credits: AP Images: 23, Achmad Ibrahim, 45, Lenny Ignelzi, 40, Mahmoud
Tawil, 14, U.S. Air Force, 17; Corbis: EPA/Justin Lane, 6, Reuters/Chip East, 4; DVIC/
U.S. Navy/MC1 Eric L. Beauregard, 27; Getty Images Inc.: Abid Katib, 31, AFP/Atta
Kenare, 30, AFP/Banaras Khan, 18, AFP/Jo Yong-Hak, 12, AFP/Liu Jin, cover, AFP/
Mandel Ngan, 20, AFP/Mustapha Ahmad, 9, AFP/Prakash Singh, 10, AFP/Shah
Marai, 39, AFP/Stan Honda, 28, AFP/Tang Chhin Sothy, 36, Paula Bronstein, 35;
Shutterstock: Cristi Matei, 15.

Library of Congress Cataloging-in-Publication Data
Bedell, J. M. (Jane M.)
  Combating terrorism / By J.M. Bedell.
    p. cm.
  Includes bibliographical references and index.
  ISBN 978-0-7565-4309-9 (library binding)
  1. Terrorism—Prevention—Juvenile literature. I. Title.
  HV6431.B3368 2010
  363.325'17—dc22   2009038908

Visit Compass Point Books on the Internet at *www.compasspointbooks.com*
or e-mail your request to *custserv@compasspointbooks.com*

Table of Contents //////////

A Constant Threat ///////////////

In the summer of 2008, a man living in New York City decided to join a terrorist group. He was angry about the war in Afghanistan and wanted to attack the United States. He soon found another man, who he thought was part of a terrorist group, and asked for his help.

The man the terrorist talked to was an informant who was working with the Federal Bureau of Investigation. The informant told an FBI agent about his meeting with the terrorist. The FBI agent asked the informant to help capture the terrorist. The informant agreed to help, and by fall he was meeting regularly with four men who had joined the terrorist group. The FBI placed hidden cameras in the house where the group met. Every discussion the men had was secretly recorded.

Suspects in a terrorist plot to blow up targets in New York were arrested in May 2009.

By April 2009, the terrorists had agreed on their targets. They chose a synagogue in the Bronx and a military plane at Stewart Air National Guard Base, near Newburgh, New York. They watched the targets, took pictures, and made detailed plans. When the plans were finished, the terrorists told the FBI informant to get them explosives and surface-to-air missiles. The informant asked the FBI for the weapons. The FBI gave him fake explosives and a missile that couldn't fly or blow up.

The terrorists never knew the

Security was tighter at synagogues and other Jewish sites in New York after a bombing plot was discovered in 2009.

weapons were fake. They thought everything was in order, and they set a date for the attacks—May 20, 2009. On that day, as the plot was set in motion, FBI agents and New York police officers swooped in and arrested all four terrorists.

Every day around the world, men and women are trying to stop terrorist attacks. They watch what possible terrorists are doing and where they are going. They look for clues that might help them find unknown terrorists. They piece together information that could help stop an attack. Peter King, a member of Congress from New York, said, "We don't know how many [terrorists] are out there, and it's why we can never let our guard down, and we have to be extremely vigilant."

A Worldwide Battle

In many parts of the world, terrorist attacks are common. Great Britain, France, South Africa, Sudan, and Russia

Constant Vigil

On May 21, 2009, the morning news reported the story of how FBI agents and New York police officers had stopped a terrorist attack. Later that day, during a speech in Washington, D.C., President Barack Obama said, "[National security] is the first thing that I think about when I wake up in the morning. It is the last thing that I think about when I go to sleep at night." He is not alone.

were combating terrorism long before the United States joined the fight. The event that pushed the United States into action happened September 11, 2001. That day terrorists attacked the World Trade Center in New York City and the Pentagon, the U.S. military headquarters,

September 11, 2001

Number killed:	2,819
Number of nations that lost citizens:	115
Jobs lost in New York because of the attacks:	146,100
Economic loss to New York City in the month after the attacks:	$105 billion
Estimated cost of rescue and cleanup:	at least $11 billion
Estimated amount of money needed to overhaul lower-Manhattan subways:	$7.5 billion
Estimated number of jobs lost at the end of 2002:	100,000 in lower Manhattan; 237,000 nationwide in the travel industry; 1.8 million total
Estimated September 11-related insurance claims paid worldwide:	$40.2 billion

near Washington, D.C. Thousands of people died in the attacks, and the recovery cost billions of dollars.

According to the National Counterterrorism Center, in 2007 there were about 14,000 terrorist attacks worldwide. They killed more than 22,000 people. The NCC is a government agency that collects terrorism-related information. Almost 90 percent of the attacks and deaths in 2007 occurred in the Middle East and South Asia. Almost 45 percent of the attacks and 60 percent of the deaths happened in Iraq.

There are two basic ways to combat terrorism. The first is to go on the offensive and try to prevent it. This is called counterterrorism. The second is to try to defend against it. This is called antiterrorism. The words *counterterrorism* and *antiterrorism* are sometimes used for one another. Although the words are defined differently, many organizations that fight terrorism fit into both categories.

The job of combating terrorism is vast, and the number of people committed to the work is huge. But no matter how successful they are, terrorism will never go away completely. It is beyond the power of any government to stop the actions of a few determined people. The best we can hope for is that the impact of a terrorist attack is small.

Iraqi firefighters battled a blaze ignited when a car bomb exploded in a Baghdad neighborhood.

WHAT IS ///////////// COUNTERTERRORISM?

The United States and other nations define counterterrorism as actions that prevent, deter, block, or respond to terrorism. Counterterrorism is taking action. Think of counterterrorism as you would a superhero. The superheroes are militaries, police forces, and other people involved in governments. They stand guard to prevent terrorists from entering their countries and to keep them from causing harm if they do enter. They track terrorists and terrorist groups no matter where they try to hide. They try to stop terrorists from carrying out attacks.

Top Indian and Pakistani security officials and diplomats met to share information as part of an effort to combat terrorism in their countries.

Counterterrorism groups have many tools to help them fight terrorism. Diplomacy and various information-gathering practices are some of the methods that are used every day.

Diplomacy

Most nations talk to one another through their diplomats. They handle problems such as finding hidden nuclear weapons or keeping

U.S. Secretary of State Hillary Clinton met with South Korean President Lee Myung-bak. The two countries have worked together to urge North Korea to stop provoking other nations with nuclear threats.

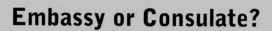

Embassy or Consulate?

An embassy is a group of people who represent their country while living in a host country. The head of an embassy is called an ambassador. He or she is the voice for the government. Embassy staff members work in an embassy building. All embassies and embassy buildings are in the capital city of the host nation.

A consulate is not as important as an embassy. Consulates are in smaller cities. Because consulates do not deal with sensitive issues about which the host country and consulate's country may disagree, an unfriendly nation may allow consulates in the country even when it refuses to accept an embassy.

Citizens who live, work, or are traveling in the host country can find help at their nation's consulate. Like embassies, consulates replace lost visas and passports, issue birth and death certificates, provide absentee ballots, and help citizens with government paperwork.

two nations from going to war. Diplomats work, sometimes for years, to find common ground and agree on treaties and alliances.

A diplomat can be any person who speaks on behalf of his or her government. These men and women combat terrorism by encouraging national leaders to hunt down and kill or capture terrorists in their own countries. They also ask that leaders support people who live in areas where terrorists are hiding, by supplying food, jobs, and medical care, and keeping schools open.

Collecting Intelligence

Information about terrorist activity is called intelligence, and there are many ways to gather it. Some is collected by diplomats. Governments friendly toward each other exchange ambassadors. The ambassadors watch and listen to what is happening in their host countries. If something important occurs, they tell their governments. Information from ambassadors helps their government's leaders make important decisions.

Ambassadors also speak for their governments. They work on such matters as trade and military activity. They also encourage cultural exchanges, such as art exhibitions and musical performances. Nations that are hostile toward each other do not exchange ambassadors. For example,

Lebanese President Michel Suleiman (left) and former U.S. Ambassador Jeffrey Feltman discussed the two countries' relationship after U.S. President Barack Obama took office.

the United States does not have an ambassador in North Korea or Iran.

Friendly nations share information. Hostile nations keep secrets. Some nations want to appear friendly, but they only share some of their secrets. Gathering information from hostile nations is the job of specially trained teams such as Britain's Secret Intelligence Service and Security Service. In the United States, organizations such as the Central Intelligence Agency and the National Security Agency collect intelligence. When it comes to stopping terrorist attacks, most Western countries work together and share the information they collect.

One way to get information about hostile countries is by using satellites. Satellite pictures can show changes that are happening

Satellites offer a safe way of gathering intelligence from dangerous areas.

on the ground. They can show the movement of soldiers, guns, machinery, airplanes, missiles, and ships. They can see whether tunnels or underground rooms are being dug. Experts can look at the pictures and see whether a nation is expanding its nuclear program or building a chemical processing plant.

Another way to gather intelligence is to listen in on telephone conversations. This is called wiretapping. In many countries, the government's use of wiretapping is questioned. Some people think it should be allowed because it helps find terrorists. Other people think it should be stopped because it invades the privacy of people who aren't involved with terrorism.

Governments also find information on the Internet. They watch chat rooms, MySpace pages, Facebook pages, blogs, Twitter, and e-mail. Terrorists can use online communication services to share information about their plans and activities.

One of the best ways to gather information is by using secret agents, also known as spies. The work they do is called espionage, which means the gathering of secret information. Nations try to secretly place spies wherever they think they can get the best information.

Spying is dangerous work. If caught, a spy can face life in prison or even be killed. Spies might work as scientists on an enemy nation's secret weapons project. They might work as employees with access to top-secret government papers. Or they could infiltrate a terrorist group. This is the hardest and most dangerous spy job. If terrorists find out a member of their group is a spy, they may torture and

The U.S. Air Force's Micro Aerial Vehicles can be as small as bumblebees and are capable of flying undetected into buildings where they can spy on terrorists.

kill him or her.

Governments might use all of these methods to find terrorists inside their borders. However, in many countries there are laws that limit how much a government can spy on its own people.

MONEY, THE MILITARY, AND WEAPONS OF MASS DESTRUCTION /////////////////////////

Nations have made long lists of people and groups that they believe are planning, committing, or supporting terrorism. The lists include more than 40 terrorist groups and are more than 400 pages long. The lists are used to help track terrorists' movements and find their money, no matter where it is hidden. If money or property is found, it's taken and used for counterterrorism efforts.

Financing Terrorism

Taking money and property from terrorists has forced many of them to find other ways to pay for their attacks. Some money comes from religious groups or charities that support their causes. Looking into how a religious group or charity spends

A Pakistani soldier stood guard near a pile of burning drugs during a ceremony to mark the fight against illegal trafficking and drug abuse.

In 2009 the FBI announced additions to its "Most Wanted Terrorists." Daniel Andreas (top right) of San Diego, California, was the first domestic terrorist added to the list.

its money is a tricky process. Many countries have laws that protect that information, and often such groups will not cooperate.

Another way terrorists get money is through money laundering. This happens when money is moved around, or "washed," so the original owner cannot be found. Money to be laundered passes through businesses, families, and sometimes governments. Hundreds of billions of dollars are laundered every year when countries trade products with one another.

Terrorists in the Middle East can hide the source of their money by using an ancient money transfer system called hawala. Money is given to a hawala broker, who passes it to another broker. The money goes from person to person through a hawala network. Hawala transactions use cash and oral promises, without any written contracts. This makes the trail of the money almost impossible to trace.

A lot of terrorist money comes from buying and selling illegal drugs. So counterterrorist groups destroy drug crops before they are harvested. They seize drugs that are exported from drug-producing countries. They find drugs that are smuggled into countries. They stop people from selling drugs and try to help those who use drugs. Any drug money that is seized is used to help victims of terrorist attacks or to fund counterterrorist efforts.

One example of a drug sale's paying for a terrorist attack happened in 2004. A commuter train in Madrid, Spain, was bombed. The attack killed 191 people and injured 1,800. One of the terrorists said the explosives used to make the bombs were paid for with $8,600 and a supply of hashish, a commonly used illegal drug.

Using Military and Police Forces

Once important information is collected, governments may call on their military for help. The military can do a lot to combat terrorism. Either alone or with the help of friendly nations, the military can block seaports, bomb terrorist hideouts, monitor terrorist movements, and find and destroy weapons. If asked they can enter a country as a peacekeeping force. As a last resort, military forces can fight a war against a terrorist nation.

When the job is tracking down or watching individual terrorists, specially trained military units can be used. Unit members, their locations, and their missions are top secret. Many countries have such units, and often they work together to combat terrorism around the world. The United States uses Special Mission Units that get their members from military groups such as Delta Force, the Navy SEALs, and the Army Rangers. Israel has the Mossad. Germany has the Grenzschutzgruppe 9. The British have a Special Air Service unit. And the French have the Groupement d'Intervention de la Gendarmerie Nationale. They respond to a crisis or conduct secret operations on land, on the sea, and in the air.

The military has an important job to do, but the world's local police officers are on the front lines daily in the fight against terrorism. Police officers walk our streets, patrol our neighborhoods, and guard important places. They follow up on leads and arrest suspected terrorists. They are the first to arrive on the scene of a terrorist attack.

In countries where terrorist groups are most active, police officers are at the greatest risk. They are threatened, captured, tortured, and even killed for their efforts to protect people from terrorists. Sometimes their loved ones are kidnapped and killed.

Tracking Weapons

Many nations try to stop the spread of regular weapons and weapons of mass destruction. Regular weapons include tanks, machine guns, assault rifles, and anti-aircraft missiles. The biggest problem with these weapons is tracking where they go once they are sold. They can move from buyer to buyer until they end up in the hands of a terrorist group. Tracking them is hard because the sales happen quickly, and the weapons are often moved across national borders.

Weapons of mass destruction are designed to kill large numbers of people. Some of them destroy property, such as buildings or even entire parts of cities. All of them are meant to cause fear and panic. WMDs can be biological weapons, such as anthrax; chemical weapons, such as sarin gas; and radiological weapons, which include nuclear weapons and smaller so-called "dirty bombs."

Anthrax is a bacterium that enters

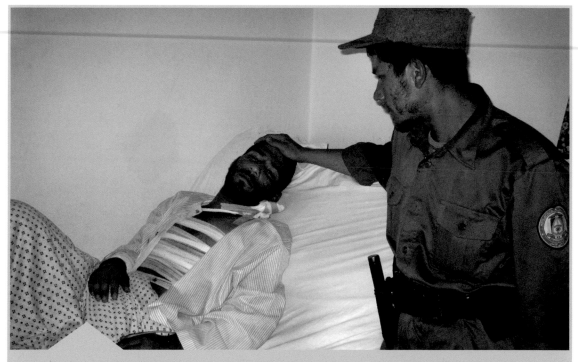

A police officer comforted an officer who was wounded in a suicide bombing of a police training field in northern Afghanistan.

the body through the skin, lungs, or mouth. It attacks the body and causes severe illness or death. Anthrax is easily spread because it attaches to any surface and floats in the air. As a weapon, it can kill many people, force the closure of buildings, and cause widespread panic.

Sarin gas is a man-made chemical that was originally used to kill insects. One application can kill thousands of people. The gas enters the body through the skin or lungs and attacks the nerves. In small doses, it can cause twitches, but in large doses it causes seizures and death. Sarin gas is dangerous because it's easy to make and easy to spread over large areas.

A dirty bomb destroys property, kills people, and spreads a small amount of radiation. The panic after the explosion and the difficulty in cleaning it up are what most affect a city. There has never been a dirty-bomb attack, but unexploded bombs have been found. Experts believe it is only a matter of time before one is used. Keeping track of these weapons is difficult because they are easy to get, fairly safe to carry, and hard to detect.

Nuclear bombs top the list as the most lethal weapons of mass destruction. But obtaining a nuclear weapon is difficult. Nuclear bombs and missiles, including their parts and fuel, are closely watched. Except for wars, the chance of a nuclear attack would increase only if the government of a nation with nuclear technology suddenly collapsed. Then the weapons could fall into terrorists' hands.

Two nations that have nuclear weapons and fragile governments are North Korea and Pakistan. No one knows who may seize power in North Korea in the future or what would happen to that country's nuclear weapons. Pakistan's government is weak and is struggling to control terrorist groups inside its borders. If one of those groups seizes power, nuclear weapons could fall into the hands of terrorists. Most nations think it is in the world's best interest to keep these nations' governments from collapsing and to find ways to end any conflict or instability.

Helping in the search for WMDs is the International Criminal Police Organization. INTERPOL, which it is often called, has its headquarters in Lyon, France. With 188 member countries, INTERPOL is the world's largest international police organization. INTERPOL trains police officers around the world to recognize and handle these weapons. It also teaches them how to prevent and prepare for any type of WMD attack.

Biological and Chemical Attacks

* **Amerithrax:** A 2001 anthrax attack in the United States. Anthrax was sent through the mail to several places, including the offices of a U.S. senator and a U.S. congressman. Five Americans died, and 17 others became sick.
* **Aum Shinrikyo attack:** A 1995 chemical attack on Tokyo, Japan. Packages containing sarin gas were placed in five Tokyo subway commuter trains. Once released, the gas killed 12 people and injured about 3,800.
* **Halabja attack:** A 1988 chemical attack on Halabja, Iraq. The Iraqi government bombed the Kurdish village with mustard gas and the nerve gases sarin, tuban, and VX. An estimated 3,200 to 5,000 people died, and 7,000 to 10,000 were injured. In the years that followed, thousands more died from the effects of this massive chemical attack.
* **Rajneeshee attack:** A 1984 salmonella attack in Oregon. It sickened 751 Americans who ate food from 10 restaurant salad bars that were deliberately contaminated. No one was killed.

SANCTIONS, SIEGES, AND BLOCKADES

Without a common definition of *terrorist* or *terrorist group*, nations often differ on how to deal with them. Some nations support terrorists with money and protection. Some refuse to hand over terrorists living within their borders. A few nations are considered terrorists themselves, and they refuse to cooperate with other nations.

In situations like these, countries use diplomacy to encourage cooperation. If diplomacy fails, then sanctions, sieges, and blockades can be used to force cooperation. Using these methods can cause problems, since nations seldom all agree on a single action. The best way to get cooperation is for a country to ask the United Nations for help.

The United Nations has 192 members that represent almost every nation on Earth. The United Nations' Security Council is composed of five permanent members and

The U.S. Navy and Coast Guard seized a ship in the Gulf of Aden, near Yemen and Somalia, that was captured by suspected pirates.

The United Nations headquarters is in New York City.

10 nonpermanent members. The Security Council makes policy decisions that involve sanctions or the use of force. Under the United Nations charter, all U.N. member nations are required to accept and carry out the decisions of the Security Council.

Sanctions

Sanctions are penalties that a country or group of countries uses to force another country to conform to international law or opinion. Sanctions can be placed against nations that give terrorists money or a safe place to hide. They can also be placed on nations that allow genocide—the killing of large numbers of people simply because they belong to a certain ethnic, religious, or other group.

One kind of sanction is putting a high tax, called a tariff, on goods imported from the wayward country. Another is limiting the amount of goods imported or exported by that country. Forbidding citizens from doing business with a country is another way to sanction. This can include selling to, buying from, and visiting that country.

In 1998 Japan and the United States sanctioned India. They were protesting India's five nuclear tests at the Pokhran test site in the Thar Desert. In the years leading up to both wars in Iraq, the United Nations placed sanctions on Iraq, trying to force it to let weapons inspectors see its nuclear weapons sites. Those sanctions ended in 2003, when the United States and its allies invaded Iraq and secured all of Iraq's weapons sites.

Today the United States has sanctions against Iran because of its support of terrorism. The United Nations has urged sanctions against a list of al-Qaida and Taliban terrorists. Because of these sanctions, all member nations are required to freeze bank accounts and stop all financial transactions either by or for the benefit of anyone on the terrorist list.

Economic Sieges

An economic siege stops just short of war. It happens when a country blocks everything from going into or out of another country. This includes food, water, and medical supplies. An economic siege can backfire. The longer a siege is in place, the more likely it is that other nations will get upset. They

Iranian President Mahmoud Ahmadinejad (left) has been criticized for human rights abuses, his country's nuclear program, and its support of terrorism.

know that women and children are going hungry and that people not involved with the country's actions are suffering as well. These countries may pressure the sanctioning nation to allow food, water, and medical supplies into the country or to end the sanctions altogether. If either of those things happens, the siege may not be effective.

In 2008 Israel began an unsuccessful economic siege against the Palestinians in the Gaza Strip. The area has been the site of conflict between the mostly Muslim Palestinians and mostly Jewish Israelis for many years. The Gaza Strip is land that Israelis say is theirs. The Palestinians disagree and say it's theirs. They want to build an independent homeland on it.

The siege was supposed to force the Palestinian government to stop shooting rockets into Israel and killing Israeli citizens. But as the siege progressed, diplomats from other countries pressured the Israeli government to end the siege.

A masked Palestinian man smuggled a cow through a tunnel to the Gaza Strip during an Israeli blockade.

Blockades

A blockade is usually used when one nation is at war with another nation. In a land blockade, soldiers patrol the borders of a country and refuse to allow anyone or anything to go in or out. A naval blockade happens at sea. Ships block all ships and boats from going into or leaving a country's ports. This stops all shipping trade and can lead to hard times within the blockaded nation.

In August 2008 Russia sent ships into the Black Sea to blockade the coast of Georgia. Russia and Georgia were fighting over possession of South Ossetia, a small region in the Caucasus Mountains. The blockade was an attempt to stop weapons from entering Georgia.

In 2009 shipping companies asked the United Nations to blockade the coast of Somalia. They wanted to stop pirates from leaving that eastern African country and seizing ships in the Gulf of Aden.

Counterterrorism uses force to weaken or destroy terrorist groups.

One problem facing counterterrorism leaders is how to handle a mission when the line between regular laws and the laws of war gets blurred. This happens in the heat of battle and usually involves harm to someone's human rights.

Another problem for counterterrorist groups happens when terrorists give wrong or misleading information to newspapers or radio and television stations. This is called propaganda or psychological warfare. It is designed to sway public opinion and gain sympathy. Counterterrorist agencies can release only a small amount of secret information and therefore are often powerless to respond.

Counterterrorism Agencies Around the World

Country	Agency	Headquarters
Australia	Special Air Service Regiment, including the Tactical Assault Group and the Offshore Assault Team; and the No. 1 Commando Regiment of the army reserve	Perth
Canada	Joint Task Force Two of the Canadian Armed Forces	Ottawa
France	Groupement d'Intervention de la Gendarmerie Nationale	Outside Versailles
Germany	Grenzschutzgruppe 9	Hangelar
	Kommando Spezialkraefte	Calw
Indonesia	Special Detachment 88	Jakarta
Israel	Sayeret Mat'kal	Sirkin Air Force and Army Base near the village of Kfar Sirkin on the Sharon Plain
	Mossad	Tel Aviv
Netherlands	Bijzondere Bijstands Eenheid, a unit of the Royal Netherlands Marine Corps	Van Braamhouck Geest Kazerne
Norway	Forsvarets Spesialkommando	Rena
Oman	Sultan's Special Forces	Muscat and Dhofar
Russia	Spetsgruppe A	Moscow
United Kingdom	Special Air Service's Special Projects Team	Credenhill
United States	Delta Force (Combat Applications Group), assisted by SEAL Team 6, the 160th SOAR team, and the CIA's Hostage Rescue Team	Fort Bragg, North Carolina
	Special Mission Units	Top secret/unknown

WHAT IS ANTITERRORISM?

Counterterrorism means offensive measures against terrorism. Counterterrorism groups find, fight, and eliminate terrorists. On the other hand, antiterrorism describes any defensive measure that reduces the exposure of people and property to terrorist attacks. This includes such things as wire mesh and concrete barriers that protect buildings and the people inside. It also includes limited help from the military or civilian police forces, such as patrols that guard buildings or areas that could be targets for terrorists.

Antiterrorism groups block terrorists from entering important places such as airports, government buildings, and weapons facilities. They stop terrorists from getting money, weapons, or people to carry out their attacks. And they try to get rid of what makes people help terrorists or become terrorists. Antiterrorism activity is like a huge roadblock. The roadblocks can be built by government agencies, nongovernment organizations, and individuals.

Protecting Human Rights

In response to the actions of Nazi Germany during World War II, the United Nations approved the Universal Declaration of Human Rights on December 10, 1948. Since then, the ideas in that document have become part of international law. Every member of the United Nations is supposed to give these rights to their citizens. If they don't, they could face sanctions or removal from the group.

The Universal Declaration of Human Rights, which includes civil rights, has been translated into 360 languages. It's celebrated each year on December 10, International Human Rights Day. Some nations don't like the ideas in the

Students in a crowded Afghan school studied in UNICEF-supplied tents and war-torn buildings as they waited for a new building to open.

document because their religion or their customs conflict with one or more of the rights. But most nations see the document as the foundation for any civilized society.

In part, antiterrorism is about building stronger societies. Antiterrorism groups introduce the ideas of individual freedom and equal justice in countries with little history of human rights, civil rights, or political participation. Antiterrorism groups hope to keep people from ever supporting or joining a terrorist group.

Nongovernment Organizations

According to the United Nations Office of Drugs and Crime, there are 112 international nongovernment organizations at work around the world

A Cambodian boy prayed in Phnom Penh, Cambodia, during the 58th anniversary of International Human Rights Day.

United Nations' List of Human Rights

The right to live free and with dignity

Freedom from slavery and forced service in any form

Freedom from torture or any cruel or degrading treatment

The right to choose, without pressure, whom one will marry

The right to own property and not have it taken away without just cause

Freedom of thought and conscience, opinion and expression; this right includes
the right to change one's mind

The rights to work, choose an employer, and be given equal pay for equal work

The right to rest and leisure, including limits on working hours and periodic
holidays with pay

United Nations' List of Civil Rights

Freedom of speech

Freedom of religion

Freedom of the press

The right to peacefully assemble

The right to participate in government either directly or through a representative

The right to choose a government through regular and fair elections, with equal
suffrage, a secret vote, and an unhindered voting procedure

The right to equality before the law and protection of the law

Freedom from random arrest, detention, or exile

The right to not be discriminated against because of gender, age, religion, race,
caste, or disability

that help in the war against terrorism. Many NGOs work in areas where the terrorists live, but the NGO members do not have military protection. NGOs can use armed security workers or other means to protect themselves.

NGOs focus on rural communities, such as small towns and villages. They build hospitals that educate doctors while tending the sick or injured. They build clinics to help women care for their babies. They dig wells, build schools, and teach farmers new and better ways to grow crops. NGOs combat terrorism by offering immediate help as well as hope for a better future. Their goal is not just to help people but also to make them less likely to become or support terrorists.

Humanitarian Groups

Humanitarian groups help people. They send food to nations hurt by drought or war. They give children shots against such diseases as smallpox, polio, and measles. They send clothing, tents, water, and other supplies to people affected by earthquakes, floods, or other disasters. They help farmers grow crops and women start small businesses. They promote education, self-reliance, and hope.

One group dedicated to helping a lot of people is the World Bank and its 186 member countries. Through the use of grants and loans, the World Bank supports education, health care, and protection for land and animals in poor countries.

Another humanitarian group is the International Red Cross. The Red Cross is quick to help whenever disaster strikes, anytime and anywhere in the world.

Human Rights Groups

All terrorist acts deny the human right to live freely and without fear. Human

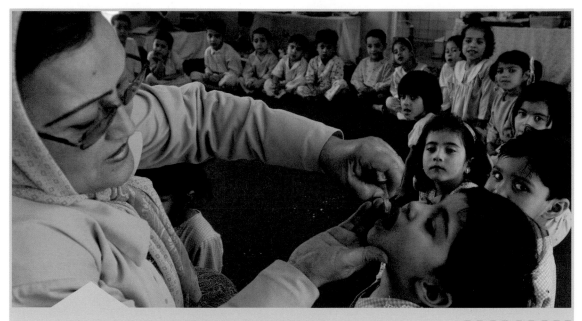

An Afghan health worker dropped polio vaccine into the mouth of a child as part of an immunization program in Kabul.

rights groups try to change the way governments think about their citizens. Instead of working for the rich, they tell government officials, help the poor. Give children education and health care. Protect women against violence. Give everyone a chance to work and take care of their families.

These and many other human rights are denied to millions of people around the world. One goal of human rights groups is to give more power to people. This, in turn, can reduce the ability of terrorist groups to recruit new members.

The United Nations Children's Fund is one of the largest human rights groups. UNICEF works in 190 countries, helping to protect the rights of children and to free them from hunger, slavery, and violence. It also encourages governments to invest in education.

RESEARCH, THE RULE OF LAW, AND ///////////// THE REFORMED

In the vast network of antiterrorism groups, many people work behind the scenes. They sit at desks, teach in classrooms, and walk village streets. One by one, they try to find ways to stop terrorists.

In an effort to understand the enemy, some people dig deep into the causes that trigger terrorist acts. They study terrorists' religious beliefs, cultures, and individual lives. They search for clues to understand what motivates a person to become a terrorist.

Others teach government leaders new ways to create, and then enforce, laws meant to protect every citizen. They do this by talking to leaders and persuading them to act.

And some people risk their lives each day to talk to people on the streets. They break down barriers. They find those who

Researchers try to develop drugs to combat radiation poisoning and other chemical and biological threats.

support terrorists and try to persuade them to stop.

Research

Some researchers combat terrorism by studying how terrorists think. They try to understand why terrorists commit violent acts. They examine how terrorists recruit new members, and how they plan and carry out attacks. Researchers share what they learn with world leaders. The information is used to help form plans to stop terrorists.

One group dedicated to research is the International Centre for Political Violence and Terrorism Research in Singapore. One of its projects is a study of the ideas that lead to and sustain extremism and terrorism. The group's goal is to find new ways to respond to and challenge radical ideas.

Researchers are studying ideas such as jihad and fatwa. *Jihad*, an Islamic word for a holy war, is used by Islamic extremists as a call to fight the Western world.

A fatwa is a ruling by an Islamic religious leader. It is supposed to be obeyed, but each believer is free to accept or reject the ruling. Researchers work with religious scholars to correctly read the original text of the Qur'an, Islam's holy book. Then they spread the correct reading of the text to as many people as possible, in as many ways as possible. Doing this, they hope, will make more Muslims reject fatwas that encourage them to support terrorists and accept those that favor peaceful ways to end conflicts.

Civil Liberties Groups

Civil liberties groups try to persuade governments to approve laws that support human rights, civil rights, and justice. In some countries, when a law is passed, civil liberties groups train police officers on how to enforce the law. They teach lawyers how to defend the law. They teach judges how to decide cases so their decisions can be used as guides in the future.

After a law is passed, civil liberties groups work hard to make sure people learn about it. The groups go from village to village, passing out pamphlets and holding meetings. They use newspapers, television, and radio to spread the word about the new law.

Civil liberties groups bring civil lawsuits against terrorists and terrorist groups. When civil liberties groups succeed, the terrorists' money goes to their victims rather than to pay for future attacks.

The National Council for Civil Liberties is a civil liberties group that has been around for more than 75 years. Based in London, England, it

Successes in Combating Terrorism

* **September 2009:** A man was arrested in Denver, Colorado, after buying large quantities of items that could be used to make bombs. Authorities found bomb-making instructions on the man's computer hard drive and believed he was building bombs to attack targets in the United States.

* **June 2007:** Four terrorists were arrested in a plot to blow up large fuel tanks at John F. Kennedy International Airport in New York City.

* **May 2007:** The FBI stopped six terrorists who had planned to kill soldiers at Fort Dix in New Jersey.

* **December 2006:** In Rockford, Illinois, a terrorist was arrested for planning an attack on a Chicago shopping mall during the holiday season.

* **August 2006:** British agents stopped a terrorist plot to blow up several passenger airplanes bound for the United States. Authorities believed the group was two or three weeks away from carrying out the plan.

works in England and Wales to defend the rights of ordinary people and hold those in power responsible for their actions.

Former Terrorists Lend a Hand

One of the best ways to combat terrorism is to work with former terrorists. They are men and women who have chosen to reject violence and commit their lives to helping others do the same. They are effective, and often successful, because they understand the ways the terrorists think, and they often live in the same towns and cities.

The former terrorists are accepted in their communities. They sit in the same coffeehouses, walk through the same markets, and worship with the terrorists and their families. As long as they are not too outspoken, everyone remains calm. An example of how this works can be found in Indonesia and Singapore. Former terrorists in both countries are helping police build trust within their communities. They are giving money to captured terrorists' families. They are helping their children get an education or jobs. When the terrorists and their families accept the help, trust grows. As trust grows, the willingness to commit acts of terror is reduced.

Will Terrorism Ever End?

It's impossible for every person, every day, to be completely safe from a terrorist attack and still live in a free society. The most we can hope for is to reduce the number of attacks, the number of people killed, and the amount of property that is damaged.

There are ways, however, to keep the terrorists from reaching their goals. Terrorists use fear to control people and destroy communities.

Police and former terrorists in Indonesia are working together to battle terrorism.

If communities are growing strong and people are living without fear, terrorism is being combated. When an attack happens and there are few or no deaths, terrorism is being combated.

When terrorists have no influence on government policy, terrorism is being combated. When communities come together and demand peace and reject violence, terrorism is being combated.

GLOSSARY

alliances—friendly agreements to work together

assets—property that can be given a value

biological weapons—weapons that use living organisms such as viruses or bacteria to cause harm or death

blockade—prevent people or goods from entering or leaving a place

broker—someone who is paid to buy, sell, or negotiate for someone else

chemical weapons—weapons made with a substance produced through the use of chemistry to cause harm or death

fatwa—legal opinion or religious decree by an Islamic leader

human rights—rights that should belong to every person, such as freedom from unlawful imprisonment and torture

infiltrate—to join an enemy's side to spy or cause some type of damage

informant—someone who gives information about another person's criminal activity to police

international—involving two or more countries or their citizens

jihad—campaign waged by Muslims in defense of the Islamic faith against people, organizations, or countries regarded as hostile to Islam

laws of war—special rules designed for times of war

propaganda—information spread to influence the thinking of people; often not completely true or fair

radiological weapons—devices that spread radioactive material to cause harm or death

sanction—punishment for breaking the law or for unacceptable behavior; may include one country's refusing to trade with another

siege—surrounding of a place in order to cut off supplies and force the surrender of those inside

terrorism—use of extreme or violent acts to create fear and achieve certain goals

ADDITIONAL RESOURCES

Further Reading

Beyer, Mark. *Homeland Security and Weapons of Mass Destruction: How Prepared Are We?* New York: Rosen Publishing Group, 2005.

Donohoe, Helen. *Terrorism: A Look at the Way the World Is Today.* North Mankato, Minn.: Stargazer Books, 2006.

Miller, Debra A., ed. *Homeland Security.* Detroit: Greenhaven Press, 2009.

Mortenson, Greg, and David Oliver Relin. *Three Cups of Tea: One Man's Mission to Fight Terrorism and Build Nations—One School at a Time.* New York: Viking, 2006.

Netanyahu, Benjamin. *Fighting Terrorism: How Democracies Can Defeat the International Terrorist Network.* New York: Farrar, Straus and Giroux, 2001.

Weinberg, Leonard. *Global Terrorism.* New York: Rosen, 2009.

Internet Sites

FactHound offers a safe, fun way to find Internet sites related to this book. All of the sites on FactHound have been researched by our staff.

Here's all you do:
Visit *www.facthound.com*
FactHound will fetch the best sites for you!

Look for other books in this series:

The History of Terrorism
Terrorist Groups
What Makes a Terrorist?

Select Bibliography

Berntsen, Gary. *Human Intelligence, Counterterrorism, and National Leadership: A Practical Guide.* Washington D.C.: Potomac Books, 2008.

Bolz, Frank Jr., Kenneth J. Dudonis, and David P. Schulz. *The Counterterrorism Handbook: Tactics, Procedures, and Techniques.* Boca Raton, Fla.: Taylor and Francis, 2005.

Byrd, Miemie Winn. *"Combating Terrorism: A Socio-Economic Strategy."* National Defense University. NDU Press. Joint Force Quarterly. Issue 41, 2nd quarter 2006, pp. 15–19. 27 August 2009. www.ndu.edu/inss/Press/jfq_pages/editions/i41/i41_forum_03.pdf

Ganor, Boaz. *The Counter-Terrorism Puzzle: A Guide for Decision Makers.* New Brunswick, N.J.: Transaction Publishers, 2005.

Turchie, Terry D., and Kathleen M. Puckett. *Hunting the American Terrorist: The FBI's War on Homegrown Terror.* Palisades, N.Y.: History Publishing Company, 2007.

Index

About the Author

J.M. Bedell teaches writing at George Fox University in Newberg, Oregon, and has written several books for young readers.